Before You Were You

by David and Jonathan Shmidt Chapman

Illustrated by Diane Nelson

Brandylane
Publishers, Inc.
Publishing books since 1985

ISBN: 978-1-953021-45-8
LCCN: 2022907238

Production managed by Jenny DeBell

Printed in the United States of America

Published by
Brandylane Publishers, Inc.
5 S. 1st Street
Richmond, Virginia 23219

Brandylane
Publishers, Inc.
Publishing books since 1985

brandylanepublishers.com

Dedicated to everyone who
helped us become a family

Before you were you,
We watched you grow
From two tiny specks
Into one embryo.

And long before that,
You were merely a dream.
A wish and a hope—
In our eyes, a bright gleam.

Would you like to know how you came to be,
Before you were you, and two I's became We?

In the heart of the city, your dads felt a spark.
It was love at first sight while we sat in the park.

From season to season,
Your dads' love did bloom.
After tons of adventures,
We became groom and groom.

4

But all of our love was too much for just two,
And that's when we knew we had to make you.
It wouldn't be easy, but the best things take time.
The view from the top is worth the whole climb.

So, what did we need?
An egg and a seed.
Counting seeds—we had plenty, but eggs? None, indeed!
"We'll need some help," we both agreed.

We wished, and we hoped.
We searched far and wide—
The missing ingredient
For someone to provide.

We thought long and hard,
Who should she be?
And then it was clear.
"It's an artist we need!"

Our artist used color and light to invent
Beautiful creations wherever she went.

We knew she'd be perfect,
But what would she say?
We asked if she'd help.
We didn't delay!

"You may not have all of the necessary parts,
But you have what's important—two very big hearts.
I'll give you my egg to give you your start
At creating this beautiful new work of art."

And just like that, she helped us conceive
The greatest gift we would ever receive.

With the help of a doctor and many a friend,
We planted our seeds in her egg . . .
The End.

"... but wait!" You might ask,
"How did I grow?
All you had then
Was a small embryo!"

Good point ... we still had steps to complete.
You hadn't yet grown a nose, eyes, lips, or feet!

So, what did we need?
A warm room called a womb.
Counting bellies—we had plenty, but wombs? None, indeed!
"We'll need some more help," we both agreed.

We wished, and we hoped.
We searched far and wide—
The missing ingredient
For someone to provide.

We thought long and hard,
Who should she be?
And then it was clear.
"A teacher!" we agreed.

She filled young minds with all that she knew—
Her classroom, a greenhouse, where each student grew.

We knew she'd be perfect,
But what would she say?
We asked if she'd help.
We didn't delay!

"You may not have all of the necessary parts,
But you have what's important—two very big hearts.
I'll give your embryo a place to hang out.
My womb will be where your baby will sprout."

And just like that, she helped us conceive
The greatest gift we would ever receive.

With the help of a doctor and many a friend,
We planted the embryo in her womb . . .
The End.

"But WAAAAIIIIIT!" You might say,
"That's it? It can't be!
What happened on the day
That I became Me?"

Well, for eight months we watched
As you blossomed and bloomed.
Our missing ingredient
Would come home to us soon.

And then, just like that,
You really couldn't wait.
You arrived a bit early—
You didn't want to be late!

You came into this world
With a face that shone bright.
You lit up the room
With a radiant light.

Your daddies held you
For the very first time.
We were finally together
After such a long climb.

And with that, we conceived our family of three . . .
With the help of an artist, a teacher, a doctor, a dozen nurses,
our family, some seeds, an egg, a womb, and many a friend . . .
The greatest gift we could ever receive.

While it may seem far-fetched, this love story is true.
That's how we became daddies
And how you became you.

The End

AUTHOR BIO

David and Jonathan Shmidt Chapman met in an elevator in Times Square, married in 2013, and dreamed of starting a family. After an incredible adventure in egg donation and gestational surrogacy, and with the help of a loving community, the couple welcomed a child into the world in 2017. Trained as artists, educators, and community leaders, David and Jonathan are passionate about creating new stories in which all children see themselves represented within the pages of children's books.

ILLUSTRATOR BIO

Diane Nelson is a professional medical illustrator. She has been an artist as long as she can remember and loves to create engaging and fun images that help the reader identify with the story. Diane is the president and art director of BIOMEDIA Corporation, a company she founded, and sole practitioner and owner of DianeNelsonStudio.com, an illustration and visual arts studio. Diane is the proud Gramma of the child who inspired this story.

www.ingramcontent.com/pod-product-compliance
Lightning Source LLC
LaVergne TN
LVHW070838080426

835511LV00025B/3477